LOSER

THOUGHTS AND WAR STORIES
FROM YEARS OF CASINO BATTLES

by Mr. Lucky

DORRANCE
PUBLISHING CO
EST. 1920
PITTSBURGH, PENNSYLVANIA 15238

Dorrance Publishing Co
585 Alpha Drive
Suite 103
Pittsburgh, PA 15238
Visit our website at *www.dorrancebookstore.com*

ISBN: 978-1-6491-3096-9
eISBN: 978-1-6480-4676-6

CONTENTS

INTRODUCTION

I have never written a book, or anything for that matter, more than a Christmas card greeting. Now I thought, wouldn't it be great if I could go to publishers with something so immensely desirable that they would be crawling over one another to market my book? But unfortunately, I did not have a scorching hot tell-all exposé about being some celebrity's secret lover or something (sorry I even brought that image up). But what I do have is a lot of experience with casinos and there are millions of people who frequent these establishments. There are millions more who may have gone once or twice, with both good and bad feelings about them. There are more who have never gone and wonder just what the deal is. And, I'm sure there are many that may or may not have ever gone to a casino but hate them. Some are just too cheap to spend even one penny on this type of entertainment. Some don't like games of chance. And some who think casinos are Satan's Dens of Evil, where any money lost goes straight towards building the express monorail to hell and any money won goes to even more debauchery, sending your life into a hopeless spiral of doom.

Whatever your perspective may be, I just want to tell about the highs and lows, joys and frustrations, and mayhem and oddities that go on in the strange world of casinos. Hopefully, this is a book for the veteran casino goers (without boring them), as well as the novice that may wonder just what the attraction is.

There will probably be more questions raised than answers found. Casinos have a way of bringing out the entire spectrum of human emotions, a few of which may actually be admirable. Of course, all of the bad characteristics are exhibited by "other" casino guests, never ourselves.

With that being said, this book will probably come off as either a perverse love story or a cry for help (or both).

On with the show!

1 | A DAY IN THE LIFE OF MR. LUCKY

Damn. Damn. Damn. It happened again.

I had been playing a $1.00 video poker machine and was losing my butt. When I get smeared by a slot machine, I usually move far away from it so if someone wins on it, I don't have to know about it. You can keep playing a machine assuming your luck will change, but often it will not and you will have to give up. I don't know why, but after I lost this time I only moved a couple of rows over to a different type of machine. Sure enough, after only a few minutes, I hear that "Jackpot Song" that machines play when someone wins something big. It is a most wonderful song if it is coming from the machine you are playing. If it is from another machine, it is a different story. The casinos think that when other people hear the happy little tune, it will encourage them to keep playing. It's signaling to them, "Hey, this person is a big winner and if you keep playing you too will win." There may be a couple of halfhearted congratulations from any surrounding people who have not yet been drained of their decency and humanity. But in reality what that tune does is cause heads to snap violently towards the direction of the music so forcefully that visits to chiropractors will be needed—while everyone at the same time all thinking in unison, *Who's the unworthy bastard that had the nerve to win instead of me?*

Anyway, I know I didn't have to even look, but I did anyway. The music was coming from the machine I was just playing and had lost a few hundred dollars at. The jackpot on this machine for a royal flush with the maximum bet ($5.00) is $4,000.00, and that's what the person won. Yes, this person who had the nerve to sit down at "my machine" and "win my jackpot."

And then, this is when those dark and despicable thoughts start to creep into my head. I consider:

Act fast, choke him out, stash him behind another machine, take his place and collect the jackpot.

The old chloroform and rag trick, take his place, claim he's just a person walking by and fainted he was so happy for me.

Rely on the fact that if I was caught I would be tried before a judge and jury of fellow casino goers and they would find me completely innocent.

Eventually, I try to snap back to reality and realize it's not worth a lengthy prison term for four grand. So I return to my current machine, slump down a little lower in my chair and plod on.

There are so many people that go to casinos and there are so many different outcomes from these trips. Some win and some lose. And then there are the few, the chosen, who battle viciously, win on occasion, but usually lose, often in the most cruel, tear-your-heart-out-and-stomp-on-it, soul-crushing ways imaginable. This is the category I, your humble servant and observer, Mr. Lucky, is here to represent.

2 | THE CRUEL REALITY

It sucks to lose. And believe me, Mr. Lucky knows how it feels to lose. Why is it when one has a successful session it's pleasing, but never quite "enough"? I know why it doesn't. It's because when you win, you're only winning back about 10% of what you just recently lost. It's insane! It's a rip-off! Oh, sorry, lost my cool there for a moment. But for Mr. Lucky and I imagine a lot of other people, it's true to some extent or another that the casino has more of your money than you have of their money. Sure, a few people win a giant progressive jackpot of some sort. They are way up in the short run but my guess is that they eventually end up giving it all back and then some.

Sometimes a losing session is not too bad—you had a lot of "play" (give and take—win a bit, lose a bit) and you got hours of entertainment for not much money. Other times, it is the worst. Go from machine to machine, machine to table, back to machine, back to table, and nothing works. An aura sets in that there is absolutely nothing (and I mean nothing!) you can do to change your miserable luck. You want to leave, but you want to break the losing streak that you know has to end. Sometimes, the decision is easily made for you. You are out of money and have to go home. Other times, you just keep trying and trying and keep failing and failing. It's just dumb bad luck but feels like so much more. You think you must be a terrible person. You go back through your entire life history, trying to remember what bad deed you did that you are now being repaid for. You get spiritual. You question spirituality. You silently beg: You whine. You get mad. You say very bad words, first to yourself and then out loud, not caring who may hear you. It ends just as it started, with results that for the most part are entirely out of your control.

But, for the Mr. Luckys of the world, tomorrow will be a new day, and the battle will resume again.

Realities of Slot Machines –

They make big money for the casinos (shocking)!

Because, obviously, they take in more money than they pay out.

They vary their payouts.

You can win on a "cold" machine and lose on a "hot" machine.

So, even if the overall result is if a machine pays out say 90% of what it takes in, there are still times when you will make money when the machine is overall "cold" but in the short term "hot."

Allow me to illustrate for you how slot machines react. It will show you how a magnificently skillful player like Mr. Lucky works his magic.

Again, let's assume a slot machine with an average payout of 90% of what it takes in. This does not mean it will be exactly 90% for the entire time.

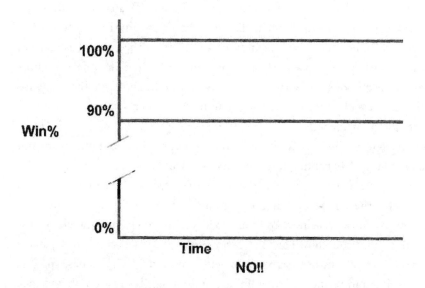

No one, not even Mr. Lucky, would play a machine where you never had a chance to make a profit.

It does also not mean the payouts will fluctuate a little bit around the 90% payout mark but still end up at 90% overall.

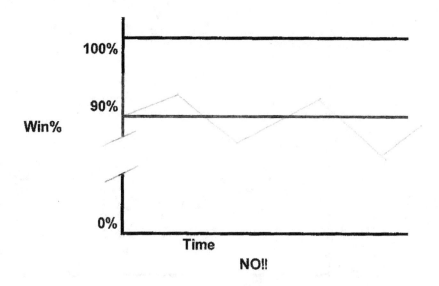

NO!!

Machines can have wide ranges of hot and cold streaks and still end up at a 90% payout rate.

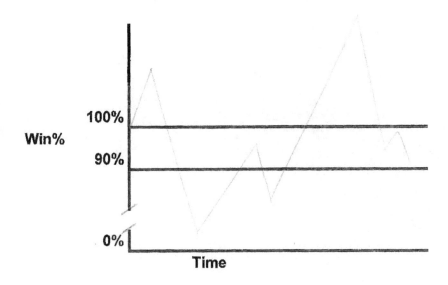

So, within these fluctuations, we have what are called "Mr. Lucky Zones." These are the times when no matter how well the machine was performing a moment ago, the minute Mr. Lucky sits down, the machine goes to hell. I can't explain it. It just happens. Every time.

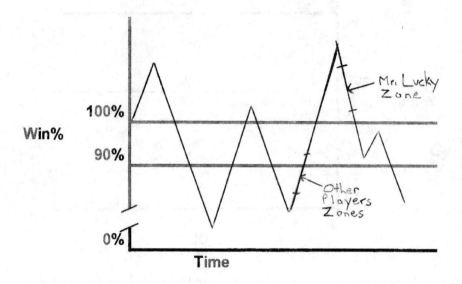

Please, make the voices in Mr. Lucky's head stop!

3 | UPS AND DOWNS

The Slump—What the hell is going on? I'm cranky, crabby, and irritable. I can't sleep and food doesn't even taste good. I've had my ass kicked sideways at the casino so many times in a row at times I've lost count. If win $10.00, I lose $100.00. If I win $100.00, I lose $1,000.00. I feel cursed. I feel it will never get better. I know it has to but when? The sick thing about it is twofold.

If you win a bit after one of these disasters, you will "reinvest" it to try to win a lot more to try to get even—and end up losing it all.

If I were to get a big win, I would just think, *It's about time.* Not overjoyed, just relief.

It sucks and it sucks the life out of you at times. But we love it, don't we?

A slump will crush your soul. It will stomp on you. It will make you say bad words. It challenges your willpower, especially when it comes to the ease of accessing money (which we will look closer at later). Oh, and add in readily available alcohol to this mix and you might be headed to therapy, counseling, or who knows what.

Winning—Funny—this section appears to be much briefer than the losing section. It is glorious when it happens. Brief moments of joy that make you wonder why this can't happen all of the time and you want more. In the back of your mind you realize it "can't happen all of the time," but I guess it is sort of like golf—even if you hit just one good shot per round, it will bring you back again for more. But as we all know, for sure, trouble is always lurking ahead.

4 | STORIES

And now for some stories. One thing is for sure. Spend any time in a casino and you will come away with plenty of stories to share. Speaking of which, see the end of the book to see how you can share some of your best stories.

Another day in the life of Mr. Lucky. I was getting smeared at the casino and had to take the "walk of shame" to the cashier cage to get some more money. I gave my driver's license to the young lady at the window and we went through the steps needed to complete the process that we had both been through hundreds of times before. She gave me back my license and receipt for the money. She then laid out the money that I had requested and counted it. Then she put it in a tidy stack to slide towards me while I was putting my license back into my wallet. Again, we had both been here a million times. When I looked back up to get my money, she took the stack and put it back into her cash drawer! We looked at each other and a moment later she said, "Oh, my gosh!" and brought it back out and gave it to me, apologizing profusely the whole time. Now sometimes it seems like Mr. Lucky is just giving his money away, but this time it almost really happened. We laughed, but I took it as another sign that it was going to be another tough night for Mr. Lucky.

Don't let it fool you—there's more going on behind the scenes at a casino than what there may appear to be. Even the small casinos are very sophisticated. They're not just bingo halls that made lots of money and expanded. Security there are more than glorified "mall cops."

One day I was playing a machine and saw a strange sight, albeit not one that was immediately noticeable. I saw what at first to be a middle-aged Asian lady walking down one of the aisles. Upon closer look, there was a casino "suit" about four feet to the right and ahead of her. Another "suit" was about four feet to the right and behind her, and a casino security officer about four feet directly behind her, all walking in unison. There was zero interaction, but something must have happened. They continued walking at a slow pace down the long aisle as far as it went, and then they turned right and kept walking as far as I could see. I assume they were headed for the exit, but it was bizarre. It was like watching the O. J. white Ford Bronco chase—this slow motion act of "offender wrangling" aimed at not dismaying the public.

Mr. Lucky has no problem making fun of himself. Such an easy target, almost impossible not to. I sat down once at an Ultimate Texas Hold'em table (card game). Mr. Lucky is a bigger guy and has a long gray beard. A guy at the table says, "Now we're joined by Burl Ives (too young? Google him)." I was then informed that a minute before this an Asian man sat down at the table and they proclaimed he was Jackie Chan. He did bear quite a resemblance to Mr. Chan. Now, for all of the celebrities for one to be compared to, Burl Ives is way, way down the list, but welcome to the life of Mr. Lucky. A woman at the table then wished she would get some good hands. The "celebrity namer" guy then said, "I wish for world peace." Mr. Lucky then took his cue from his celebrity doppelganger and said, "Well, then I guess I wish for a Holly Jolly Fucking Christmas (again, if you didn't know, that is the title of Mr. Ives' hit song from many years ago without the F-word, obviously)!" This got quite a laugh. Mr. Lucky then proceeded to lose 90% of his hands and received another of many beatings where it seems like his testicles had been ripped out and stomped on by sumo wrestlers. Some days it is just difficult for Mr. Lucky to stay positive. And so it goes....

5 | GLOSSARY OF SOME TERMS

Next we should look at a few of the definitions of the most common casino features.

Slot Machines – The most common of casino big money makers. This army of R2D2-looking bastards go "beep" and "ding" and cast their spell on the masses, eventually turning them into zombies.

Video Poker Slot Machines – An evil subgenre of slot machine that lets you either hold or discard your original cards, making you think that you actually have a say in the outcome of the result. Foolish humans!

Blackjack – A relatively simple game when—played "correctly"—gives you one of the best games in the casino to get a 100% payback (supposedly about 50.5% for the house and 49.5% for the player). That's about the best a player can hope for. Again, that is under perfect conditions. Guess what? Casinos are not perfect conditions. Add in new players, dumb players, drunk players, and the fact that your name is Mr. Lucky, and you're in for a rough time.

Keno – Long odds to win, but with a chance to win relatively large amounts by betting fairly small is enticing to many people. The lower-stakes Keno is usually in a smoky corner of the casino. You will know where it is immediately by the constant "bink, bink, bink, bink" sound that casts such a trance like spell over the players. Keno players seem to have great endurance. They will sit and push the button for hours, as long as their supply of cigs hold out.

Casino Cash Card – Once you have gotten a regular casino players card, you can get a casino cash card. These little gems replace the "old-fashioned" way of getting additional money by writing checks. As long as you have the money in your bank account when the cash card goes to collect, you're good. And then the more you use it, the higher your cash withdrawal limit can be. Let's see—take a casino patron, add in a little bit of a gambling issue, maybe a little alcohol, and a card where they can get $5,000.00 no problem regardless of whether they have a million dollars or $2.00 in the bank. What could go wrong, right?

ATM – Ah, the good old ATM. Ready to serve at a moment's notice. But here's the deal. Even though you are using an ATM inside of a casino—where you will more than likely spend most or all of it—you are still charged the transaction fees. Come on, casinos! You could at least pick up those fees for you to get a chance to make more money. Okay, so the person who can hopefully afford it, they withdraw $500.00 and get charged a $4.00 transaction fee. It sucks but that's life. The poor devil who lost the last penny they came with and really can't afford to lose any more but has three more hours to wait before their bus arrives to take them back home, they break down and withdraw $40.00 from the ATM and get charged the same $4.00 transaction fee (this burns my biscuits—no, it pisses me off)!

Now we can put some casino terms under the microscope for a closer look.

Money you bring from home to a casino – This is the money you feel comfortable with to spend as entertainment even if you lose it. It is still more than what you should bring, but what the heck!

ATM – Where you go after you have lost the money you brought with you from home for entertainment. At the ATM, you withdraw any remaining money you have left for the month.

The Cage (or Cashier) – The place where you take your Casino Cash Card and withdraw all of next month's available income. There is a rumor that people even also come to the cage and get paid for chips and slot payout slips they have won. To date, this rumor is still unverified.

Then, when all else fails, you can get money from your credit card at the cage (as opposed to from an ATM) – This is where you can get money from your credit card if you qualify (and these are people who usually want large amounts of money) for ridiculously high fees. I think they can run a couple hundred dollars on $600.00-$700.00. These people then receive their money accompanied by a card with the Gamblers Anonymous hotline phone number on it. If they have the money, God bless them. But, if not, yikes.

The dreaded 1099 – If you have an individual win (on one spin or one bonus game) and you win $1,200.00 or more, the law requires a 1099 to be issued. This is used to report this income on your tax form. Diabolical slot machines just coincidently have big winning amounts of $1,200.00 (not $1,199.00). Everyone freaks out about winning $1,200.00. First of all, taxes smaxes, Mr. Lucky would damn well welcome a $1,200.00 win (or any amount)! The main thing to remember is that you can write off an amount up to your documented gambling losses on your Federal tax return. So, if you had $5,000.00 in 1099s and $9,000.00 in losses, you would report the $5,000.00 as income and then declare $5,000.00 as losses. This isn't a total win, but it sure helps. This may as well be called the Mr. Lucky Consolation Prize. Mr. Lucky uses this scenario in many years. This is about the only reason doing taxes is not too painful. I have never cheated on my taxes, ever. I always have more losses than reportable winnings. Mr. Lucky is a good guy. But Mr. Lucky would really, really like the opportunity to cheat and claim excess losses due to the fact that there were so damn much winnings. Mr. Lucky is often delusional.

6 | CASINO STUFF

Casinos have their players cards, which again are another thing of genius working for them. You put $1,000.00 through their slot machines and you earn $10.00 in "Free" slot play. Yippee! You also earn points for getting smeared playing table games. Double yippee! And then you will get specials mailed to you for more "Free" play on certain days and times. My God! How can they shower all of these goodies on their players and still be in business!?

I do have to confess, though, if you are going to go and spend the money, you may as well get a little bit back for your effort. It's better than nothing. I've had several "free" meals that cost me $400.00. It helps, but not much.

What I don't understand are the people who are regulars at casinos who do not get the player cards. You'll be sitting at a blackjack table and the floor will ask if they have a players card. "Ohhh, nooo," they will respond, similar to the response someone would give if they were asked if they spit on the American flag or kicked little puppies. The thing that gets me is that they seem to have this deep distrust of what the casino will do with their information. But I'm willing to bet (surprise!) that these same people do all of their banking, bill paying, etc., online, where, of course, you have no worries at all about the safety of your personal information. I guess Mr. Lucky will take his chances and at least get a free buffet now and then.

Casino employees can be a mixed bag. It's so very important to me that the employees are nice and at the very minimum at least "seem" interested. There's nothing worse than being at a blackjack table in a rural casino with one other player at the table and they are a farmer, and the dealer is also a rural type. They couldn't care less about what is happening at the table. They are way too wrapped up in what type of bug-resistant seed to buy next spring. Dealers, also please don't be yawning, looking constantly at your watch, taking smug pleasure in beating the players and taking their money (you may be surprised, but trust me, this has happened way more than once), or any other behavior that may take away from the entertainment. If you are friendly and invested in the game, I will also tip you and we can hopefully have some fun together. I think happy dealers are a sign of good working conditions.

Another sneaky deal is that casinos give out merchandise to their card holders. Just show up on a certain day and spend some money and get that day's gift. Some gifts aren't too bad, but for what some people will come in and lose to get, say, a pillow is well worth it for the casino. I have to hand it to the Native American casinos that this is a great revenge for getting a lousy $24.00 in trinkets for Manhattan all those years ago. One casino didn't have enough space for all of the merchandise they were giving away, so they had a tent just outside the front door with a sign on it that read "Redemption Center." I took it in a different way. I took it as a sign that I should go inside, drop to my knees, and beg for redemption! It would probably cause a scene, but Mr. Lucky needs all of the help he can get.

There seems to be a different mindset in casinos. Hey, chips aren't "money." It's just a couple of chips. Well, no. It turns out it's your utility bill payment.

Another type of diabolical slot machine is the one that's "only a penny" machine. The problem is that it has 40 to 50 lines and you can play multiple increments, so you could spend up to $5.00 a spin. You don't have to, but you want to increase your odds of winning, don't you? So, you play 50 lines at two credits per line, which is $1.00 per spin. Hey, you're going to "win" something on most every spin. You win on two lines! You win four credits on line seven and eight credits on line 34. Nice!

Ahh, wait a minute. You won 12 credits, or 12¢. You bet $1.00. What's wrong with this picture? The machine wants you to think you won, but you got your ass kicked! As you continue to play and continue to "win," your money evaporates. But you're seeing lights and hearing bells, just like a winner is supposed to. Sure, you can occasionally win a larger payout, but seemingly never enough to make a profit. It's pure evil genius.

Another brilliant scam is the online casino. Play for "Fun"! No real money! Earn more coins the more you play! These are often very realistic, as you get your butt kicked just like the real machines. They give you a bunch of free money to start with, but with these machines they usually require you to bet a large amount also, $200.00 minimum bet for example. So with each spin your "free" money goes quickly. But wait—if you run out of free play, no worries. You can buy more. But this time with real f-ing money! You can get $80,000.00 in play for $20.00. Or you can get $6,000,000 in play for $500.00. It costs you a real $500.00 (U.S. American money)!!

7 | MORE STORIES

Things are backwards in the alternative universe of casinos. You can be drunk, high, whatever to play a slot machine. All you have to do is push the damn button. But I don't see that too much. I see it much more at the table games like blackjack, etc. Where you have to think at least a little bit. Never good results when you are drunk, high, tweaking like mad, etc. Kids, don't do drugs and bring a lot of money to a casino! Quick aside—Though sometimes I wonder if I should do a little meth just for a week or two. My house is a mess and it would supposedly cause me to stay up for days on end with so much energy I would be cleaning the bathroom tile grout with a toothbrush. Okay, relax. I'm only kidding. But boy, the house would look great!

Even the legal stuff can get you sometimes. Once, at a lower-stakes black-jack table, things were going okay so everyone at the table remained there for a longer period of time. One guy ordered a coffee and another and another and another. The waitress was coming around quite frequently. As she came by, "Coffee! Coffee!" he was shouting while shaking. I could almost hear his teeth grinding.

Anyone who has played table games has been at a table with a know-it-all. After every lost hand, "Why didn't you stand? We would have won." I'm pretty sure everyone makes the correct play AFTER the hand is over! I'm also pretty sure everyone at the table is trying to win. Casinos don't need to plant "coolers" at the tables (but, if they did, it would be a perfect job for ol Mr. Lucky here with his unique skills. Just saying...).

At blackjack, I've been blamed for just about everything, though I play what would be considered almost perfectly "by the book" strategy-wise. If you know blackjack, the hand of soft 18 (ace and 7) is the most misplayed hand. It is either 8 or 18. People almost always stand with their "18" when they should often hit or double down. Obviously, nothing works every time. But it is sweet when the dealer has a face card showing and you have a soft 18 and hit for a 3 to make 21. In this case, you should be hitting to improve your hand because—news flash—18 does not beat 20. Well, if it doesn't work and we all lose, there's silence for a second, then a finger or two points to the 18, a couple of tsking noises, and on and on. If it would have worked—no credit at all! I tell ya, no respect, no respect at all.

Once, I was at a blackjack table with two other players. I was in the first spot. I had a 10 and a 2 for 12. The second player had 15, I believe, and the last player had 18. The dealer was showing a 2. The "book" says to hit a 12 against a 2 and I did and I got a 2 for 14. Not great, but I didn't bust and was still in the game. The two other players both stood (correctly). The dealer turned over his hole card and it was a face, making his hand 12. So he has to hit and gets a 7 for 19, beating all of us. Now, if you have been paying attention, you'll notice me taking a 2 did not change the outcome of the hand. If I would have stood, the dealer would have had 21, beating us all either way. Well, the third player went ballistic on me. He called me every name in the book for taking a hit. I tried to explain that it did not change the outcome. He would have none of it and continued on with his assault. Now I quickly thought that this calls for some quick-witted action, some kind of snappy and beautiful retort that would diffuse the situation. Ahh, I had it. I turned to my abuser and said, "Fuck you (Ahh, what a wit Mr. Lucky has)." Well, he freaked out. This eventually snapped the pit boss out of her standing coma with the ruckus. She rushed over to the table and told ME that everyone just needs to play their own hands! Once again, fairness and casinos do not seem to coexist in harmony.

⑧ | SERIOUS (MOSTLY)

I don't claim to have any expertise in the field of addiction. I agree gambling can be an illness, and I think it is just bad luck if you suffer from an addiction. It doesn't make you a bad person. I don't like cigarettes. I don't drink too much and could survive if I could never have a drink again. I like to gamble. I enjoy gambling. If I had no money, I would not gamble and would survive, though probably not be very happy. Why that seems to be my vice of choice, I have no idea. People do a lot of bad things to support habits of hard drugs, etc. But lots of bad things are done by people in the grasp of a gambling addiction. They will steal from the school PTA bake sale proceeds. They will lie, cheat, and steal from their spouses and friends. And, yes, there are instances of people who will murder to support their gambling habit. Most people cannot (and should not) be able to grasp this concept that when someone is addicted, it would have that great of a hold on you, but it does. Thank God the most I do is bitch a little bit and maybe give a quick elbow to a slot machine when no one is looking. The reality is that casinos can be a fine way to innocently pass time. They can do a little damage to your wallet but, hopefully, not be a problem. Casinos do walk a fine line. They want to "lure" in customers and use tricks to hook them to get as much money as they can from them. This is sort of like cigarette companies (or drug dealers). They can potentially ruin people. But, if they ruin all of their customers, guess what—no more customers. What is the answer? I'm not sure.

One final point. Another reality is that casinos are not as "glamorous" as they are often depicted. A penny slot player on a three-day two-night casino junket will not end up drinking champagne and snorting blow off of naked high-priced call girls (sorry to burst that bubble).

9 | CASINO FEATURES

There are all kinds of casinos. Some are state run, others by big corporations, and many not in Las Vegas but in almost every state. Many are casinos operated by Native Americans. I have nothing but respect for Native American casinos. They all seem well run and welcoming. These casinos have provided a much needed source of income to some places that have had very little opportunities. Sadly, the most profitable casinos are nearer to larger populations and the number of tribe members are smaller, so the tremendous profit is split only a very few number of ways. This makes a few people ridiculously wealthy, while the smaller casinos on the more remote reservations help but not as much. I do believe most, if not all, of these casinos reinvest proceeds back to their entire population. I'm sure there could be a long discussion about people receiving money but without training, jobs, etc., but we can hope far more good than bad comes from this.

After being serious, I need to get back on track. One of my favorite episodes of *South Park* was when the local Native American tribe casinos wanted to make a super highway right through the middle of South Park so customers could get to the casino faster. This would cause the ruin of downtown South Park. The townspeople were protesting, but the casino had a secret weapon. This episode was made during an outbreak of the illness SARS—which originated in China. So, in the usual politically incorrect South Park way, the casino would take their handwoven rugs and have a back room where they took Chinese guys and rubbed them all over the rugs. The whole town was sick.

Yes, they were actually taking Chinese guys and rubbing them on the rugs (c'mon—the show is animated so they can do things exactly like this)! Well, everything worked out in the end (I'm sure Kenny was killed for fans of the show). Hopefully, we can all be good sports and have a laugh once in a while. Oh, and by the way, thank goodness for the good folks of *South Park* that they had the special antidote for their sickness. Spoiler alert—The special antidote was Seven-Up and saltine crackers.

I don't know if casinos know it or not, but they often seem to be giving their customers the needle by how they flaunt all of the money they make. These seem to constantly be making needless renovations just so they have something to spend all of their money on. Now the hotel rooms are nice, though I'm pretty easy to please. Just be clean and have a good bed. And the food is usually good also. I don't think I have ever had a really bad meal.

We have touched on comps before, but here's a little more. Getting a comp is better than a sharp stick in the eye. It lures you in to come and play more, but someone has to win these drawings; why not me (could it be that my name is Mr. Lucky, he says, dripping in sarcasm)? People go nuts for the giveaways. There are also cleverly items that go together as a set, so you have to go every week for all four weeks of the month to get the complete set (go first week for the pillow, second week for the pillowcase, third week for the sheets, and fourth week for the blanket). If this mad genius brain-power could be harnessed for things other than how to suck people into casinos, I feel we would have cures for many more diseases and be on our way towards world peace.

As far as entertainment goes, I myself have never really seen a great show at a casino. Now, I have to amend this slightly, due to the fact that some casinos have built large outdoor amphitheaters which will draw in more top-name entertainment. Otherwise, it is a lot of "veteran" acts where it is often a quick money grab for them. If it is a big name, expect to pay a big price for a ticket. If it is a "lesser" act, they seem to fall into three categories:

1. A comeback from waaaay back
2. A comeback no one was really clamoring for
3. "I thought he was dead"

Oh, and don't forget the groups from way back who still have the rights to the group's name, but the closest thing to an original member is it has the lead singer's cousin's barber in it.

Casinos supposedly pump extra oxygen into their air (at least in Las Vegas) and some give you free drinks. They do everything they can to keep you both up and not thinking clearly. A great way to get you to empty your pockets.

A change for the better is when casinos went from actual coins to paper tickets for slot machines. When the actual coins were paid out, they were filthy. You would see older ladies wearing gloves on their "money-scooping" hand to stay clean. They looked like a Michael Jackson fan club meeting. Coins caused those metal on metal filings to get on everything. Oh, and add that to the smart asses who would flick their cigarette ashes into the coin bins. Never wear white after Labor Day. Never wear white to a casino, ever!

Speaking of the days when the slot machines dispensed coins, that meant they had to be refilled with their treasure every so often when they ran out. Casinos then had more slot employees for this exact job, but finding one was often a challenge. When a machine ran out, it had a light on top of it which would flash to alert someone that it was in need of a refill. Well, like there seems to be in every place of employment, there are some employees who work harder to try to get out of work than the simple act of just doing the work. You would be sitting at your machine with its light flashing—even when it was not very busy—and wait for a fill. Some employees would walk by, staring straight ahead sort of like a zombie, fearful of making any eye contact with you or your machine. Maybe it was just my imagination, but I thought I would see some with their hand up to the sides of their faces like blinders on a horse. Now, of course, there were many fine and helpful employees, but heck, whoever remembers them, right?

The slot attendants would also get some paper printouts from the slot machines that they needed to deliver back to their "command center." One day, I was playing a slot machine when a slot attendant walked by. He had a large bunch of these paper printouts in his back pocket. As he went by, some of them fell out. He kept walking, unaware of what had happened. I picked them up and started walking after him. "Sir," I said. No reaction. I sped up a bit to get a little closer to him. He must have spotted me out of the corner of his eye. He sped up. I swear I could feel the aura of his body shouting, "Oh my God!

It's a patron and they actually want me to HELP them with a slot machine." So I sped up. Then he sped up. It basically got to the point where we were having the Olympic gold medal speed walking finals right there in the casino. I finally kicked it into a bit of a trot to be able to tap him on the shoulder. He reluctantly stopped. I said, "Here. You dropped this," and stuck the paperwork into his hand. He kind of blankly stared at me and grunted, "Okay." I'm sure he was relieved he was not being asked to do anything. Mr. Lucky does not plan on doing cardio workouts when he visits a casino.

10 | POKER

Poker rooms exist in various types of gambling establishments. The huge wave of popularity for poker may have ebbed a bit, but it has left us with a large group of superstar wannabes. You have the Phil Helmuth know-it-alls, the young guns with the dark glasses and the hoodies pulled tight on their head, and every other type of TV stereotype you can think of. They are all excellent poker players and a chump like Mr. Lucky has no chance, even at the lowest-ante level limits. You hear them talk, "How did you do last night?" and "See you tomorrow." Poker rooms are places to avoid. They are where people like Mr. Lucky are looked at like hungry Dobermans look at a porkchop. It doesn't end well for the porkchop.

11 | SCAMS

You can rest assured that when there are games of chance where people dream of winning big money, there will be people who come up with ways to get these people to spend even more of their money. They do this by selling pipedream so-called secrets and systems of how to win big that are total BS. These scams—er, I mean "Fabulous Secret Systems That Guarantee That You Will Win a Fortune!"—are everywhere.

The ridiculous claims these scams make are too good to be true because they aren't true! They prey on the blind hope of desperate people who want to get that edge on the casino that no one can get. Mr. Lucky is ashamed to admit he has purchased one or two of these dumb rip-offs, thinking even if there is just one little speck of helpful information in it would be enough to give me some success. Shame on Mr. Lucky.

Many of these scams come with "money-back guarantees," usually if you can "show" that their system didn't work (like of course you are going to send them a garbage bag full of losing horse race tickets—no problem)! Even when I knew I had been had by these scams, I never sent back in for a refund. I was too embarrassed to do so. I felt a need to suffer the penalty for being so stupid (not sure—it might be a Northern European heritage—Lutheran thing. Oh, well).

These scams use special names to excite you –

The M.O.T. Method for Lotteries (I have no fricking idea what the hell M.O.T. is)

Tell-All Book for Slot and Poker Machines (it obviously didn't tell enough)

Cyber Slot 21-K (this has got to be good, right? Sounds like you are getting help from robots)

G-14 System for Horse Racing (I guess I should have waited for the G-15 System)

Progressive Predictable Numbered System (this was worthless—totally predictable)

Banned Wealth Nabber System (Yes, this should be banned!)

Most all of these "success manuals" could probably be summed up on one page or less. They are padded with filler - like silly charts and graphs and other useless information. You wouldn't be happy spending $20.00 to $100.00 for a one-page product (though I sure as hell would be if the damned thing worked)!

These scammers are laughing all the way to the bank. I hate them. I secretly want to be one of them.

These scams cover three of the main ways of gambling for the most part. These are lotteries, horse racing, and slot machines. Let's look at lotteries first. These scams claim they can predict the outcomes of the upcoming lotteries and improve your chances of winning so you "can't" lose. Now, I'm no rocket scientist, I did take a couple of statistics courses, and this doesn't make sense. Results from previous lottery drawings do not influence the results of future lottery drawings. Each drawing is an independent event. Just like if you flip a coin and it comes up heads ten times in a row, the chances of it being heads the next time is 50/50 (unless you are a cheating coin tosser). This search for trends is the same reason why casinos display the outcomes of the previous plays on roulette and baccarat. People feel they can "sense the flow" of the game. Mr. Lucky says good luck.

Horse betting is something I firmly and truly believe does benefit from good and educated analysis of the information that is available. There are many smart horse players out there. But there are also scammers willing to sell you some of the lamest (horse joke!) information known to man. Some are so complicated it would take you two hours just to handicap one race. One "system" had you go through the Daily Racing Form and assign points to about 20 different factors on each horse—forget it! Another had you assign points if a horse was going up in class, finished the last race within 3-1/2 lengths of the winner, was adding weight, if the jockey was left handed, it was a Wednesday, if the temperature was between 76° and 78°, and on and on. One even had this gem of advice. It said, basically, when all else fails, go with the consensus pick from the Daily Racing Form. Well, no shit, Sherlock! Sure glad I paid for that great insider strategy.

Now for slot machines. These are beauties. These scams love sequences and patterns. They are all like: Play one coin, then, two if you get back three, or one if you don't. Play three the next spin. Then play as follows –

1-2-1-1-4-3-1-4-5, or 1-2-2-3-3-2-2-1-1. Always some specific pattern. All I know is I would win when I had one coin in and lose when I had five coins in. I do not know anyone who has had any success with any of these scams. I would love to hear from someone who has.

Of course these scams tell you the slots send out "secret signals," and you need to know how to read these signals to "coax" the winnings out. So you need to use a specific coin and win sequence. If you get exactly two coins in six spins in your sequence, you had a good machine. If not, I guess you're screwed. Then what? Don't know. Go to the bar.

This one slot scam takes the cake. I need to spend a little more time on it:

- You start by scouting out the casino floor
- Next, you quadrant it off into sections of about 50 machines each (I swear to God this is real)
- Note how many are occupied and how many are vacant
- Note how many men are playing and how many women (?)
- Observe the average length of time a person spends at each machine
- Note how many wins
- Then, take all of this information and multiply it by the "secret coefficients" that are provided to you

Well, if by now you haven't been thrown out for either:

- Loitering
- Stalking
- Harassment
- General Weirdness

I guess you then try to play the machines!

All I know is this:

- Luck is everything!
- You have to be there at the right time
- You have to be at the right machine, or
- You have to be at the right table, and
- You have to have the right-sized bankroll

If all of these things are right, very good things are bound to happen. If not, it can range from still pretty good to keep all sharp objects away from me.

The randomness is why secret systems and sequences are BS, but that is what also make people think there is some master plan to unlock big wins. By randomness I mean:

- I have won two $4,000.00 royal flushes on video poker machines on the same night
- Two four-of-a-kinds on video poker on back-to-back spins
- Won 19 out of 20 blackjack hands
- Won 300-plus bonus spins on a slot machine

But, I have also:

- Lost hundreds and hundreds of dollars on slot machines
- Lost over 90% of my blackjack hands for long stretches of time
- Never gotten a single bonus spin for weeks
- It all goes to prove, if you go to casinos often enough, you will lose plenty but you will win sometimes!

12 | PEOPLE

When you go to a casino, you are going to see a lot of people of all types from all walks of life. It should be fun, but we know casinos can sometimes bring out the worst in people. I think it is great that a casino can be a place for elderly or disabled people to spend some time and get out and have some fun. It's something to do, just don't blow the whole Social Security check. There's nothing worse than having to go home to a cat food sandwich for lunch!

Now sometimes things do get a bit out of whack. Like when someone is wheeling their oxygen tank behind them and repeatedly removing their mask so they can smoke cigarettes like a chimney. And what's the deal with smokers who play slot machines? They hit a bonus and immediately light up like it is just after sex, just sitting there in some post-orgasmic bliss. This has happened more than once but I was sitting next to a lady with the oxygen mask and smoking heavily. She hit a bonus, took a big hit of her cigarette, and in a voice like Moms Mabley (too young again? Google her) said, "Ohh, that was a good one, honey." I guess whatever floats your boat.

Unfortunately, I've seen quite a few uncomfortable moments between couples if they are not on the same page. Many arguments. "We're leaving!" "No, we're not!" "Yes, we are!" "No, we're not!" "Fine, I'm going to the car!" "Fine, go to the car!" "Hey, remember I drove!" "Oh, shit!" It can go on forever. Good and honest people will turn into the worst liars and deceivers. One couple was playing slots and the man had run out of money on his machine and the woman had about $5.00 left on hers. He said, "Let's go." She said, "Okay. I'll just play what's left on this machine." The man said, "Okay, I'll go to the restroom and be right back." He leaves and she promptly loses the last $5.00. I knew what was next. She did the guilty look over both shoulders to see if he was coming and then went into her purse and put another $100.00 into the machine. He came back and said, "Let's go." She replied in her best fibbing voice, "But look, I just won. I'm going to play a little longer." He wasn't happy, but he left and she continued playing. I'm sure this continued until he probably blew a gasket.

Once, while playing in the high-stakes blackjack area, a woman came up to a man who was playing at the table I was at. She whispered something in his ear. He said, "What! You ran out of money! How could you?" He continued to fume for a moment and then he said to her, "Okay. Then go to the ATM and get some more money with your card." She leaned in and again whispered into his ear. "What!?" he said again, this time even louder. "You've spent your ATM limit too?!" He was steaming. She gave him the sad face and he reluctantly went into his pocket and gave her some money. After she was out of earshot, he exclaimed, "I should have just kept with the prostitutes. It would have been so much cheaper." Me thinks this marriage is on some very shaky ground.

I have a special place in my heart for all of my fellow gamblers, but especially for the ones of Southeast Asian heritage. I know gambling is very big in their culture and casinos are smart to cater to this portion of their clientele. Many times, it is more than just a trip to a casino. It is often a family affair, with mom, dad, the kids, grandpa, and grandma (by the way, a lot of Asian "grandmas" are stone-cold killers on the blackjack tables—they really know their stuff)! Casinos are also meeting places for social gatherings and a place for friends to gather and socialize.

One time I was at a blackjack table and the shoe had ended and the dealer was hand shuffling the new shoe. It was just myself and a Southeast Asian gentleman at the table. As a way to pass time while he was shuffling, the dealer was trying to good-naturedly guess what nationality the man was. "Viet Nam?" the dealer asked. Neither the dealer nor I knew just how much English the man knew. The man shyly shook his head no. "Okay. Laos?" the dealer asked next. Again the man shook his head no. "Okay then, Cambodia?" the dealer concluded confidently. Once again, the man shyly shook his head no. The dealer then said, "I don't get it. I'm usually really good at guessing people's nationalities." He then said, "Okay, so where are you from?" The man's face immediately lit up and with a proud beaming face said, "Rochester (MN)!" The dealer almost spilled the six decks of cards he was shuffling all over the floor he was laughing so hard. Just a little communication problem can make for a fun story.

Another time I was at a blackjack table with a young Southeast Asian man, two young Southeast Asian ladies, and a young female Southeast Asian dealer. Now, sometimes it can seem like Asian men can be a little bit sexist, by the way they may gruffly talk or motion to a woman. Sometimes they may be a little too direct as in this case. The man was saying to the dealer in a not very politically correct way, "C'mon, honey. Give me blackjack." The dealer basically ignored him. Before the next hand, he said to the dealer, "Honey, give me blackjack and I'll take you to dinner." The dealer, who was 100% Asian, but I'm sure was born and spent her whole life in the U.S., was definitely not impressed. She said, "Oh, yeah? Where will you take me?" The man replied, "I take you to Red Lobster!" The dealer then emphatically said, "I hate Red Lobster." That slowed my man's roll down a little bit, but undeterred, he turned his attention to the other two young Southeast Asian ladies. In his native language he said to them, "Blah, blah, blah, blah (sorry, don't know the language to be able to translate it)." The two ladies looked at each other and began rapidly talking back and forth, "Blah, blah, blah." They then stopped and turned to the man and shouted in unison, "EEWWW!!" The man, undaunted, said, "That not EEWWW. That HOT!!" The ladies excitedly talked to each other and turned and responded again in unison, "EEWWW!" I can only conclude that my man's intentions were less than honorable.

Moving on, I was sitting next to a young guy playing slots. Every time he lost he would spit on the machine. I did a double take since I couldn't believe it. He was just being a total jerk. I mentioned it to a casino employee, and being ever so helpful he said there is nothing he can do about it. The slot player was with a young lady, to whom I said, "You must be very proud." She didn't respond, but even she knew what a tool he was. So please, ladies and gents, please, please wash your hands often if you venture into a casino.

Here's a quick one. A guy who I assume had been playing (and losing) for a while came to the blackjack table I was at. He put down what appeared to be the last of his money of about $20.00 for his bet. Of course, he lost. He took both fists and slammed them as hard as he could on the table while shouting, "Fucking Indians!" Everyone's chips on the table flew in the air in what seemed to be in slow motion before crashing down in piles. My guess is Native American casino or not, this guy's luck would have been the same.

Casinos can sure bring out the worst traits in people. I was sitting at a slot machine and there was a man playing the machine to the left of me and another man playing the machine to the left of him. We were playing along and probably both losing. I saw out of the corner of my eye the man to the left of me reached into his pocket for some more money. He pulled out what was probably a $20.00 and put it into the machine. But then I also caught a glimpse of what I thought was something else fall out of his left pocket. In a snap, the man to his left reached down and grabbed whatever it was. The next thing I hear is the man to the left of me say, "Hey! That's my $100.00 bill!" The other man says, "No, it's not." The first man says, "Yes, it is. Give it back!" The second man said, "No." Now, here, of all places, this should have been very easy to resolve. There are cameras covering every square inch of the casino floor and all he needed to do was call over an employee and they would call "upstairs" to check the tape. For some reason, the first man did not do this. He kept asking several times and the second man just blew him off. Not only that, he had the cajones to remain there and keep playing his machine. Finally, to my great surprise, the first man said, "Look, I'll give you $40.00 if you give it back." The second man said, "Okay," and the deal took place—WTF! Mr. Lucky will be damned if he would lose money that way—like a pussy. Mr. Lucky loses his money the admirable and macho way. He loses it on slot machines where little elves and pink balloons stop on the wrong lines to crush his soul once again.

Casinos are great places to make new friends. Once, there was a small Arab man and a large African-American man standing outside of the high-stakes blackjack room. The Arab man was saying, "No. No. You are very stupid." The African-American man said, "Man, I'm gonna F-you up." The Arab man responded, "No. You are stupid, very stupid." To which the African-American man said, "I'm really gonna F-you up " Casinos are great places for all of us to come together—all ages, genders, races, religions, etc.—to all bond together for the common good of mankind and to unite behind the universal concept that it is always someone else's fault if we lose at blackjack!

Ultimate Texas Hold'em is a table game that is basically the same as Texas Hold'em but you are only playing against the dealer. Sounds easy, but of course the odds and payouts make it like any other table game where the house has an advantage. An older man came to the table where I was playing. In this game, if you want to play your hand, you need to place four different bets at a minimum of $5.00 per bet. He bet $20.00 and lost his first hand. He bet $20.00 and lost his second hand, all the time while not saying one word. Casinos wisely have cup holders with tabs that go under the rail to keep people from spilling their drinks. After he lost the second hand, the man grabbed one of the plastic cup holders and threw it into the front of the table, again while not uttering one word, and left. It hit my leg and bounced around for a while. Unfortunately, my only hope of getting any money out of a casino would have been if the cup holder had shattered and razor-like shards would have stuck in my leg so I could have sued. No such luck once again for Mr. Lucky.

There are a couple of other just unpleasant sorts that frequent casinos. One group are the people who see when you hit a nice win or jackpot. They don't care if you are $5,000.00 down, they only know you won something so you have money. They come up and ask for a few bucks, "I'm out of gas." "It's my birthday," etc. Come on. Casinos need to do a good job of finding these people and telling them to leave. One of the lower scams was when I was playing a slot machine and a guy came up to me and said he was a veteran and had come on a bus and had an hour or so wait until the bus would leave. He asked me for $5.00 for a beer he could at least have while waiting. I gave in. Probably two hours later, my "friend" didn't recognize me right away and started his same pitch. I told him to get lost. Trying to scam people by saying you are a veteran is the lowest of the low.

13 | CASINO FACTS AND TRIVIA

What is the world's biggest gambling destination in terms of revenue?

    - Macau, China. Three times bigger than Las Vegas.

* * * * * * * * * * * * * * * * *

Archie Karas once turned $50 into a $40 million bankroll. In 1992, he was broke, coming to Las Vegas with just $50. He got a $10,000 loan from a friend and built his bankroll through a combination of poker, pool, and craps. By 1995 he had a bankroll worth $40 million. He would lose all of his money at the Binion's craps tables. Mr. Lucky has a new hero.

* * * * * * * * * * * * * * * * *

Patricia DeMauro held the record for the longest craps rolling streak at 154 rolls. She played for four hours and 18 minutes before finally losing a roll. The odds of this happening are 1 in 1.56 trillion.

* * * * * * * * * * * * * * * * *

What was the name of the world's first casino?
- Casino di Venezia in Venice, Italy, 1638. (There is no truth to the rumor that Frank Sinatra and Don Rickles headlined there.)

* * * * * * * * * * * * * * * * *

The numbers on a Roulette wheel (1-36) add up to 666. Thank you, Satan.

* * * * * * * * * * * * * * * * *

Frederick W. Smith, founder and CEO of FedEx, saved his company by gambling in Las Vegas. He took FedEx's last $5,000 there and won $27,000 gambling on blackjack, paying the company's $24,000 fuel bill.

* * * * * * * * * * * * * * * * *

The sandwich was invented by John Montague, Earl of Sandwich, because he didn't want to leave the casino table to eat!

* * * * * * * * * * * * * * * * *

There's a subterraneous world with over 1,000 residents living just below the Las Vegas Strip. These storm drain dwellers have made subterranean homes in the over 200 miles of flood tunnels.

I'll end this chapter on that cheery note.

14 | RIP-OFF

If you are still reading this, first of all, thank you. Second, if you have probably figured out that Mr. Lucky can also be very adept at being Mr. Idiot. Therefore, it should not come as a great surprise to you that the "great" Mr. Lucky got ripped off once. Looking back on it, it seems impossible that it happened, but it did. I was playing a slot machine and a guy next to me struck up a conversation. He seemed normal, normal looking, normally dressed, normal everything. He said he let his son borrow his pickup so he could move some furniture, which left him stranded at the casino for about another three hours and he had run out of money. So on we talked and I finished playing the machine I was on.

Then, for some reason, it just happened. We made an agreement that I would lend him some money. He would provide his name, address, and phone number. It was "bad" timing, because it was one of the few times I actually had a fairly decent bankroll on me. Well, we did that and started playing machines next to each other. I, of course, lost and he—just being in the sphere of influence of Mr. Lucky—lost as well.

Again, I don't know why, we kept playing, meaning I obviously lent him more money. We lost and I said that's it. The guy was still urging me for more money. I said no and then something really weird happened. He asked again for me to lend him some more money. He then went into his wallet and handed me his Social Security card! You're all now obviously thinking, *You idiot! It's obviously fake!* But, you know, if you are a man (and not a young man) and you see with your own eyes how he dug waaay into a deep dark corner of his wallet and had to pry it out like some of the things I have in my wallet that have not seen the light of day for years and years, this was the real thing, signed and dated many years ago. I had no doubt. Who in the hell would give someone their Social Security card?

Well, dumbfounded, I lent him some more money. Shockingly, this did not work out well either. After agreeing to meet the next day to pay me back, the excuses started to come: "I'm stuck at work." "My bank transaction got delayed." On and on. I was at ultimatum time. I told him, "Meet me at McDonald's tomorrow or else." Or else what? Who knows. Oh, I also went online and found my "friend's" mugshot for a prior fraud he committed!

Here's where I'm not sure if I pleased or angered the Big Guy Above. I vowed to myself I was going to leave his Social Security card on a table at McDonald's, since he again did not show up. I wanted the worst criminals in the world to pick that card up and do many fraudulent things with it. Or I was going to go home and find every public place on the Internet and publish his Social Security number to the world to hopefully go on a shopping spree. But I didn't. The Big Guy Above was probably yelling at me, "Do it, you pussy!" But I didn't. It didn't mean I wasn't mad. I called him (surprise—I got his answering machine) and I called him every name in the book. I called that prick a rotten six-letter word six-letter word, a dirty four-letter word six-letter word, and everything else I could think of. Surprisingly, I got a call a couple of hours later. It was him, yelling at me and being indignant that I had called him these names! Incredible. Of course, he said he would send the money to me that day. And of course he did not.

Again, I probably wussed out, but I had enough. I mailed him back his Social Security card. I even called him and asked if he got it (which he did). He again said the money was on its way but it never came. For what it was worth, I talked to the casino security and they said they had other complaints about this same guy and said he was banned but were still looking for him if he ever came back. So, Mr. Lucky learned a lesson the hard way.

As a final thought on this, I still have a beautiful color copy of his Social Security card and could weaponize his Social Security number at any time I wanted to, but I know I won't. That doesn't mean I won't ever run into him some day. Mr. Lucky definitely remembers what you look like. Mr. Lucky does not like you. Mr. Lucky will hurt you. Bad.

15 | EVEN MORE STORIES

Enough with that downer. On to more stories! We all know that some people are just plain lucky. A lucky person with a big bankroll becomes an even luckier person. You hear the stories: "Well, I was down $1,000.00 but I just had a hunch this machine would turn hot so I put in another $1,000.00 and ended up winning $10,000.00." Well, hooray for you. Or another great feel-good story: "After you left that machine I put in $20.00 and won $900.00." Or "You should have been here last night." Please pass me the aspirin.

As we've said before, there are all kinds of slot players and all types of betters. One time when I was playing a slot machine, there was an elderly lady playing the machine next to me. Nothing unusual about that. She was playing a penny machine but like most penny machines that means about 30 lines with an option to bet from one to 10 cents per line. What caught my eye was she was playing just one line at one penny per spin. Now nobody plays just one line! But she was. She was intently glued to each spin she played. She would lose one penny, lose one penny, lose one penny, lose one penny, and then hit on her one line and win three cents. And when she "won," her face would light up, she would sit up straight and clasp her hand over her head and shake them from side to side, just as if she had just knocked out Mohammad Ali! Never has so little money caused so much joy. When you are this happy when you win means you will not be very happy when you lose. She was losing more than she was winning, which in her case meant she was down about 30 cents after 15 minutes. A lady who I assumed was her daughter came by after a while. The lady next to me was just as intense during every spin as she was when she started. The daughter said to her, "Are you ready to go home?" Without losing her death stare at her screen she shouted, "No! Get lost!" Now that's commitment.

Everyone will have days where they lose at a casino but some people lose control to the point where it puts them in a really bad spot. One day I was walking towards the front of a casino and a woman was just coming out. She was crying. I guess we have established that I must look like a mark so she came up to me. She said, "I lost all my money and my car is out of gas and I need to pick up my children in 30 minutes and I don't know what I'm going to do." You may disagree, but this seemed like the real deal. Even when I got took the other times there were little "signals" in my mind that gave me doubt to the authenticity of those other stories. This woman was genuinely dismayed, and looked like a Keno player who had the worst luck of her life and just overspent. I gave her $10.00 and actually felt okay about it. She thanked me and headed directly to the parking lot (not back into the casino, where we would have had a problem).

Another time I was driving out of a casino parking lot and was waiting for the stoplight to turn green. There was a minivan in front of me and I noticed something strange. There was an odd rocking motion to it but I could not see inside from where I was. The light changed to green and we both proceed up to the next stoplight. I had now gotten beside the minivan when we got to the red light. I could now see what was causing the movement in the vehicle. The woman driving it was alone in the car. She was punching herself in the side of her head so hard that her minivan would rock back and forth with each blow. The light turned green and off she went, bludgeoning herself as she drove away. We've all had days like that. Thankfully, Mr. Lucky does not like pain.

One time I was playing blackjack and there was one other person at the table. It was a lady who the dealer seemed to be quite familiar with. He asked her, "Don't you usually play Pai Gow?" She said yes, but was just doing something different. I would soon find out just exactly what she meant by "different." She played some hands normally, but many not so much. On all of the hands where she got, say 13 or 14, and the dealer was showing a 4, 5, or 6, she hemmed and hawed and agonized over each one. Again basic blackjack strategy says when the dealer has 4, 5, or 6, he has a good chance to bust. So, if you have 13 or 14, it's a no brainer to stay. Each hand, "Oh, my. Maybe I should hit. Or, maybe I should stay? Hmm." She was basically just thinking (kind of) out loud. Quite often, she would hit, causing us both to lose, naturally. I remained silent, occasionally exchanging forlorn eyeball rolls with the dealer. This went on, without there ever being any interaction between me and this woman. About the 15th time this same situation came up of her having 14 against the dealer's 16, she turned to me out of the blue and said, "Well, what do you think, Grandpa!?" What the hell! Where did this come from? After a moment, I responded to her with a single word. "Surrender," I said (for those of you who do not know, surrender is where you forfeit half of your bet right on the spot, regardless of the outcome of the hand). It's usually only done when the player has 16 and the dealer is showing a 10 or a face card, where you would expect the dealer to have 20. So if you would have hit you would probably bust and if you stay your 16 will lose. At least if you surrender you get half of your bet back instead of nothing. Of course, her situation was one where you would never surrender. But at that point, my comment of surrender was not necessarily a recommendation of blackjack strategy. It was more a recommendation of life strategy. Surrender this hand. Surrender any thoughts of ever winning. Surrender control of all meaningful assets. Surrender from life. I'm sure she was not looking for that extensive of a life evaluation, but she got one anyways. Of course, she had no idea of what surrender was and probably hit and we both probably lost again. When she was finally done playing, I asked her, "How old are you?" She replied 66 (which just happened to be two years older than Mr. Lucky was when this happened). Grandpa, my ass.

Most all "regular" slot machines are based on the same premise, just with different symbols, bonuses, and so forth. With most of them, you need some combination of from three to five "bonus" symbols to get you into the bonus round. This usually consists of a certain number of free games or wins where the amounts are multiplied, etc. One time a friend and myself were playing one machine together, putting in more money to hopefully try to win more (hey, you gotta try everything). This was a few years ago and we were playing a Dick Clark *American Bandstand* machine. Casinos know that people love to play machines based on current TV shows, etc. They have *Willy Wonka* machines and *The Walking Dead* machines, etc. Anyway, this *American Bandstand* machine had symbols that you needed to line up like jukeboxes, records, and so forth, with a picture of Dick Clark representing the bonus symbol you need at least three of to get to the bonus. Well, we were having our usual bad luck with this machine (like all of them) giving you two of the three bonus symbols you need for the bonus (usually on the first two columns) but never the third. This went on and on, and after the umpteenth time we got nothing, my friend shouted, "I want DICK!" I turned to him and said, "Don't look now, but there's a guy in an ascot and a silk shirt sashaying his way over here." Mr. Lucky is ashamed to say he sometimes does not follow the rules of political correctness if it causes him to miss out on a cheap laugh.

Video poker has an option to double up your win. You accomplish this by selecting the double-up option and the left-hand card on the screen is shown. You have to pick from the remaining four cards a card that is higher than the one showing (if it is the same, it is a tie). Now, you may be thinking, what if the card that is shown is an ace? Exactly. You're screwed! Or, if you are Mr. Lucky, the card that is shown is a four and three of the other four cards are higher than a four and the other one is a deuce. Guess which one Mr. Lucky picks? Needless to say, this diabolical enticement is not an environment in which Mr. Lucky thrives in. Simply put, I couldn't win a double-up even with a gun to my head. Of course, others have good luck. I've seen people win big with a few well-timed double-ups.

I saw a guy play a $1.00 video poker machine. He was only betting $1.00. He won and doubled up. He won that double-up and did it again. And again and again and again. He kept winning. He successfully doubled up nine times to turn his one dollar into $512.00 (1,2,4,8… 256, 512). And he cashed out and left. What a concept.

Speaking of doubling up, there was the time I was waiting while a friend I was with was in the restroom. An older gent was playing a video poker machine near where I was standing. When you win, some of these machines display the question on its screen: "Double Up?" He had just started playing and, lo and behold, got four of a kind. This was a 25-cent machine and with maximum credits played was a nice win (in the $60.00 to $100.00 range). So the machine displayed the question asking him if he wanted to risk his win and double up. A button on the left flashed "Yes" and a button on the right flashed "No." The gent was obviously a novice and was confused. He sat there with a puzzled look on his face. Anyone would see he was the kind of player who would NEVER double up, but he didn't know what to do. Mr. Lucky, always ready to save the day, went over. I explained what he was seeing. I clearly showed him the two buttons. I asked if he wanted to double up and he said no. I again clearly pointed to the "No" button and told him to push that. He promptly stuck his finger out and blew right past the "No" button and inexplicably pressed "Yes." I briefly thought, *You dummy*. But then thought maybe it's fate and a deuce will show up as his card to beat. He'll double up and be a happy camper. Well, surprise. An ace showed up as the card to beat. He sat there totally confused as to what had happened. I was going to yell at him for not paying attention and that's what he deserved, but he looked so confused and vacant I decided against that. Before anything is said, I'm moonwalking backwards at a brisk pace. When my friend came out of the restroom, I said, "Let's go." He said, "What?" I said, "Never mind. Just let's go." Even when Mr. Lucky tries to help, he and everyone and everything he comes in contact with suffers.

Some bad losers compound things by just being total boors (hey, aren't you proud of me for not calling them assholes?). When you are Mr. Lucky, at least you have learned to lose with decency and elan. Nothing worse than being at a blackjack table with some smart guy whose cards total 12 and he's asking the dealer for a face card (to give him 22 and obviously lose). Or the player who busts and loudly says to the dealer, "Thank you!" There are bad vibes when someone like that is at your table and you need to move.

The first time I was at a horse track was probably sometime in the early 1980s. My friend and I were betting $2.00 "show" bets and "won" the first two races by betting on the favorites. This meant a solid 40-cent profit on our high-stakes bets on each of the first two races. We were laughing and having a good old time. Before the third race, we were looking at the program. A man came up behind us and asked us who we liked in the next race. He obviously had seen our reactions to the first two races and interpreted it to think that we really had some kind of clue that we knew what we were doing. We tried to compose ourselves and indicated we needed to do some more research into the race, but the favorite "probably looked pretty good." When the man left, I looked at him again and then realized that he was Mike Lynn, the General Manager of the Minnesota Vikings at that time. If only he knew what a couple of schmucks he was asking for race advice from! By the way, I can't remember if our "insider advice" paid off or not.

16 | MR. LUCKY MUSINGS

I guess one must just accept their lot in life. Mr. Lucky has been known as a "good sport" and a "lovable loser." There are worse things to be called but just for once, I would like to be the ridiculously lucky asshole who can't lose and amass obscene fortunes. The one who wins at everything and receives all the awards. And at the awards ceremony, I could smugly proclaim, "I would like to thank all of the little people I stepped on and over on my way to screwing everyone for this award." We know this will never happen, though, and Mr. Lucky will just have to be satisfied with being a "good sport." That's okay, I guess.

I have lost for months on end. I have lost on slot machines so many spins in a row that I can't count that high. I have lost 90-plus percent of my hands playing blackjack, seemingly impossible to do. I know it is worse than really bad when even blackjack dealers who have seen it all are speechless. They wish me their deepest sympathy, apologize, and feel genuinely bad. But still not as bad as I do.

Then, the next time you go and win. There's just some strange mojo, juju, booga booga, or whatever when you gamble. You lose 10 times in a row and then the next time you with two $4,000.00 royal flush payouts on the same night. Weird.

The further I get into this and the more I write, I notice the more crude and obscene my language becomes. That should tell me something. Frustration. Just like when I'm at a casino in person. Some machines seem like you could play them for 10 years and never get a win. And stubborn me. I keep playing and getting nothing. I start by thinking bad thoughts. *Damn machine. I'll teach you who the boss is.* Then it keeps going. My thoughts have moved on to begging and pleading. "C'mon, buddy. Just give me one nice win. Even if I'm still down I won't hold it against you." Then, the anger begins to seep out. Big audible sighs. Then, "Oh, for Christ's sake! Come on!" Working up to total contempt and hatred. Out loud I'm muttering, "That's right, you son of a bitch. Keep it up, you piece of shit!" Almost out of money, I'm thinking, *The sign at the door said no guns allowed inside but I wish I had smuggled that ball peen hammer in. I'd show this bastard machine who the boss is!* Out of money, totally defeated, dominated, eviscerated, humiliated, and any other "-ateds" you can think of, I slink off, totally crushed. I vow I will never set foot within 100 yards of this machine ever again. I swear I hear the machine say as I walk away, "See ya next time." And I know the damn thing is probably right.

When things get really bad, my mind drifts off to a bad place. *I've got it*, I think to myself. Since there are no cameras in the bathrooms of casinos, I'll wait for a time I am alone in there, lay down, claim an injury, and sue to make big money. The only way to make money at a casino. Yes, it's come to this.

17 | FINAL THOUGHTS

Who knows what the future holds for casinos. I think they will be just fine. I'm sure there will be many more people to come similar to myself (even though I did not sire a little Mr. Lucky Jr.). I do wonder about the younger generation. Are they more into playing video games instead of gambling? I hear stories of young people going to Las Vegas, but mainly to party and not so much to gamble. Just not sure about this wacky younger generation (Boy, do I sound old. Stay off my lawn!). When younger people do go gambling, I do believe in beginner's luck. I've seen it too many times. A kid at a blackjack table without a clue will win the strangest hands and make money. This may be a curse in the long run, but enjoy it while you can. I know money is more plentiful to an 18-year-old in 2019 than days of yore, but they seem way too willing to put a couple hundred dollars in play. Hard to fathom.

I truly hope Mr. Lucky's tales of woe and misfortune have lessened the pain of any of your casino misfortunes. See, there really are other people who have worse luck than you.

Mr. Lucky wishes he could guarantee nothing but good luck to all, but let's get real. "They" will get us all in the end.

Mr. Lucky would love to hear about any casino tales any of you have experienced. Good or bad, funny or sad, wild or weird (especially). I want them all.

Please send them to:

>   Mr. Lucky
>   P.O. Box 201614
>   Bloomington, MN 55420

We will publish all of the good ones in a follow-up book. And, if we publish your story, we will send you $50.00. Really!!!

CPSIA information can be obtained
at www.ICGtesting.com
Printed in the USA
BVHW040758120521
607049BV00009B/2353